LEOPARDS

EYE TO EYE WITH BIG CATS

Jason Cooper

Rourke

Publishing LLC

Vero Beach, Florida 32964

www.rourkepublishing.com

PHOTO CREDITS: Photo on page 17 © Ahup and Manoj Shah/Animals Animals; all other photos © Lynn M. Stone.

Cover Photo: *Leopards live in a wide variety of habitats in Africa and Asia, including snowy mountains.*

Editor: Frank Sloan

Cover design by Nicola Stratford

Library of Congress Cataloging-in-Publication Data

Cooper, Jason, 1942-
  Leopards / Jason Cooper.
      p. cm. — (Eye to eye with big cats)
Includes bibliographical references (p.   ).
  ISBN 1-58952-404-7 (hardcover)
  1. Leopard—Juvenile literature. [1. Leopard.] I. Title. II. Series.

QL737.C23 C6746 2002
599.75—dc21
                                                        2002003653

Printed in the USA

CG/CG

TABLE OF CONTENTS

The Leopard   5

The Leopard's Relatives   6

What Leopards Look Like   9

Where Leopards Live   11

How Leopards Live   14

Leopard Cubs   16

Predator and Prey   19

Leopards and People   20

The Future of Leopards   22

Glossary   23

Index   24

Further Reading/Websites to Visit   24

THE LEOPARD

The leopard (*Panthera pardus*) is a big, spotted cat. Many of them live in Africa and Asia. Leopards lead very secret lives, so they are difficult to see in the wild.

Unlike many large cats, leopards have done well in surviving changes to their **habitats**, or homes. This ability makes them the most **adaptable** of the big cats.

Always alert, a leopard rests in the snow.

THE LEOPARD'S RELATIVES

The leopard is a member of the **feline**, or cat, family. Although it is much larger, the leopard is related to the common house cat. The jaguar of South America is the leopard's closest relative. The leopard is one of the cats that roar.

The snow leopard (*Panthera uncia*) is found in central Asia. It is not the same as the spotted leopard. It does have spots, but the snow leopard does not roar. It lives in cold, rocky mountains.

The rare snow leopard is a different kind of big cat than the spotted leopard.

WHAT LEOPARDS LOOK LIKE

Most leopards have both solid black spots and circular spots on their yellowish fur. There are some leopards that are almost all black. Sometimes these are known as black panthers. Black panthers and spotted leopards can come from the same litter.

The biggest leopards are about 9 feet (2.7 meters) long. They may weigh as much as 170 pounds (77 kilograms). Most leopards weigh about 100 pounds (45.3 kilograms).

With a snarl, a black leopard shows off its killing weapons.

WHERE LEOPARDS LIVE

Leopards live in nearly all of Africa and much of Asia. They are found in India, Iran, China, Russia, Arabia, Israel, Kenya, and South Africa.

Leopards live in forests, grasslands, swampy areas, and deserts. These are their habitats. Both spotted leopards and black panthers are well camouflaged in their habitats.

This leopard lives on the plains of East Africa.

A leopard growls over its kill, a topi antelope that weighs more than its killer.

Keen eyes help a leopard find prey even in poor light.

HOW LEOPARDS LIVE

Like other big cats, leopards spend much of their time resting or hunting. They like to climb and leap. Leopards don't like water, but they swim well when they have to.

Leopards usually travel alone. They move quietly and carefully. They have good eyesight and hearing. They are active all the time, but sometimes more at night.

A leopard bounds from a rock ledge.

LEOPARD CUBS

A mother leopard usually has two or three cubs. They are born blind, usually in a well hidden place. The mother takes care of her babies. The male leopard almost never helps her.

When the cubs are about three months old, they learn to follow their mother on hunts. A few weeks later they begin killing on their own. However, the cubs stay with their mother for up to two years before leaving her.

Playful cubs frolic on a fallen tree stump.

PREDATOR AND PREY

Leopards are **predators**, or hunters. A leopard feeds on other animals, its **prey**. The leopard usually hunts by stalking. Then it leaps from hiding and goes for its victim's throat.

Leopards are strong animals. African leopards usually can drag even a heavy animal up into a tree. There the leopard is safe from other animals. Leopards, however, can be killed by lions, tigers, or wild dogs.

This African leopard is nervously watching for lions. The antelope it has killed is too big and heavy to drag up a tree trunk.

LEOPARDS AND PEOPLE

Leopards have fascinated people for hundreds of years. Early people told **legends** about how the leopard got its spots.

Leopards are very secretive. Most people don't see them except in zoos, circuses, and wildlife **preserves**. Still, leopards are respected and feared.

The leopard's habitat has shrunk, putting survival of the leopard in danger.

THE FUTURE OF LEOPARDS

Many leopards have been killed for their valuable fur. And farmers fear the leopard's attacks on other animals and kill them. Sometimes the farmers put poison on dead animals and the leopard will eat the poison and die.

As the leopard's habitat shrinks, the number of leopards is shrinking as well. They are adaptable and have learned how to live with the changes. Because of this, leopards are able to survive.

GLOSSARY

adaptable (uh DAP tuh bul) — able to adjust to certain conditions

habitats (HAB uh tatz) — the home areas of animals

feline (FEE line) — of the cat family

legends (LEJ undz) — stories that have been told over time

predators (PRED uh turz) — animals that kill other animals for food

preserves (pree ZERVZ) — areas where wild animals are protected from humans

prey (PRAY) — an animal that is hunted for food by another animal

INDEX

Africa   5, 11
Asia   5, 11
black panthers   9
feline   6
habitats   5, 11, 22
jaguar   6

leopard cubs   16
predators   19
preserves   20
prey   19
snow leopard   6

Further Reading

Johnston, Marianne. *Snow Leopards and Their Babies*. Rosen Publishing Group, 1999
St. Pierre, Stephanie. *Leopards*. Heinemann Library, 2001
Schaefer, Lola M. *Leopards: Spotted Hunters*. Bridgestone, 2002

Websites To Visit

http://leopardsetc.com/
http://awf.org/wildlives/147

About The Author

Jason Cooper has written several children's books about a variety of topics for Rourke Publishing, including recent series *China Discovery* and *American Landmarks*. Cooper travels widely to gather information for his books. Two of his favorite travel destinations are Alaska and the Far East.